INDIA

Julie Murray

VISIT US AT
www.abdopublishing.com

Published by ABDO Publishing Company, PO Box 398166, Minneapolis, MN 55439.

Printed in the United States of America, North Mankato, Minnesota.
032013
092013

♻ PRINTED ON RECYCLED PAPER

Coordinating Series Editor: Rochelle Baltzer
Editor: Sarah Tieck
Contributing Editors: Megan M. Gunderson, Marcia Zappa
Graphic Design: Adam Craven
Cover Photograph: *Shutterstock*: Mukul Banerjee.
Interior Photographs/Illustrations: *AP Photo*: Keystone, Peter Klaunzer (p. 17), John Mummert (p. 33); *Getty Images*: Sattish Bate/Hindustan Times via Getty Images (p. 27), Amos Chapple (p. 21), Daily Herald Archive/SSPL (p. 31), PRAKASH SINGH/AFP (p. 19); *Glow Images*: Heritage Imagestate (p. 16), JTB Photo (p. 29), ml-foto/F1online (p. 29), SuperStock (p. 34); *iStockphoto*: ©iStockphoto.com/kastock (p. 38), ©iStockphoto.com/narvikk (p. 9); *Shutterstock*: bitan310 (p. 37), Colette3 (p. 23), Distagon (p. 11), David Evison (pp. 15, 35), f9photos (p. 13), Globe Turner (pp. 19, 38), Joe Gough (p. 27), GreenTree (p. 11), Matej Hudovernik (p. 35), imagedb.com (p. 34), jcsmilly (p. 23), Mikhail Nekrasov (p. 35), paul prescott (p. 25), Nickolay Stanev (p. 9), Waj (p. 5).

Country population and area figures taken from the CIA World Factbook.

Library of Congress Control Number: 2013932150

Cataloging-in-Publication Data

Murray, Julie.
India / Julie Murray.
    p. cm. -- (Explore the countries)
ISBN 978-1-61783-812-5 (lib. bdg.)
1. India--Juvenile literature. I. Title.
954--dc23
                                                      2013932150

INDIA

Contents

AROUND THE WORLD

Our world has many countries. Each country has different land. It also has its own rich history. And, the people have their own languages and ways of life.

India is a country in Asia. What do you know about India? Let's learn more about this place and its story!

Did You Know?

Hindi and English are both official languages of India. But, hundreds of different languages are spoken throughout the country.

The Taj Mahal is a famous building in India. An Indian ruler had it built in the 1600s to honor his wife.

PASSPORT TO INDIA

India is in southern Asia. Six countries are on its borders. India is also on the Indian Ocean.

India has a total area of 1,269,219 square miles (3,287,263 sq km). It has the highest population of any country except China. More than 1.2 billion people live there.

WHERE IN THE WORLD?

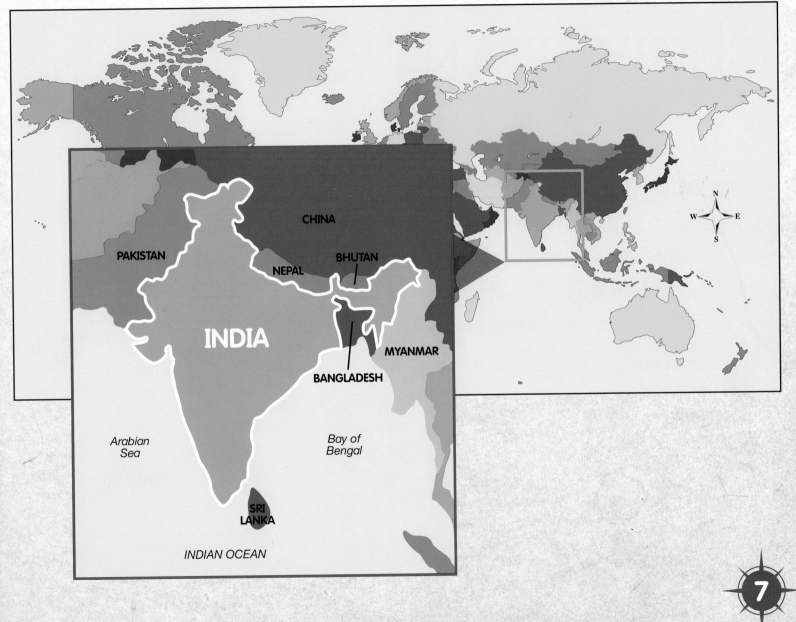

CHINA

PAKISTAN

NEPAL

BHUTAN

INDIA

MYANMAR

BANGLADESH

*Arabian
Sea*

*Bay of
Bengal*

SRI
LANKA

INDIAN OCEAN

N
W E
S

IMPORTANT CITIES

New Delhi is India's **capital**. It has about 250,000 people. It is known for its many trees and beautiful gardens. It was built near the city of Delhi starting in 1912. At that time, Great Britain ruled India.

Mumbai is India's largest city. It is home to about 12.5 million people. Once called Bombay, it is on an island in the Arabian Sea. Mumbai is known as a center of business. And, many movies are made there.

SAY IT

Delhi
DEH-lee

Mumbai
MUHM-beye

INDIA

Delhi
New Delhi ★

• Mumbai

Bengaluru •

The Presidential House is in New Delhi. This palace is home to India's president and has more than 300 rooms!

Since the 1700s, Mumbai has been an important port for Asia.

Delhi is India's second-largest city. It is home to about 11 million people. Delhi is located on the Yumana River. It is a center for **transportation** for India.

Bengaluru is the third-largest city in India, with about 8.5 million people. It is also known as Bangalore. Bengaluru is home to businesses that make aircraft and computers. And, many colleges are located there.

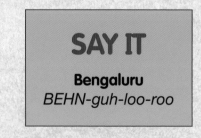

SAY IT

Bengaluru
BEHN-guh-loo-roo

Some parts of Delhi were built in the 1600s. These areas have ancient walls and gates. There are also many narrow, winding streets.

The Vidhana Soudha is in Bengaluru. It is a large government building.

11

INDIA IN HISTORY

The first **civilization** in India started more than 4,000 years ago in the Indus Valley. These people had systems of writing and measuring! Over the years, other groups came to India and took over. India became known as a rich country because of its fabrics, gold, and spices.

Ruins of ancient cities have been found in India.

In the late 1400s, Europeans arrived in India by sea. They saw its value because of the rich spice trade. For about 200 years, the British East India Company and Great Britain ruled India. India fought back and won independence in 1947.

Today, India works to overcome its struggles. Many people live in areas called slums or shantytowns. Some have no electricity, running water, or bathrooms. There are also problems with people who disagree on government and religion.

 Did You Know?

The British East India Company formed in 1600. It allowed Great Britain to trade goods with India and other places in Asia.

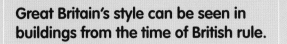

Great Britain's style can be seen in buildings from the time of British rule.

Timeline

1498

Vasco da Gama was the first
European to arrive in India by sea.

About 380

Chandra Gupta II became **emperor**
of Northern India. He ruled as part of
the Gupta **dynasty**. Many consider
this India's golden age because of
growth in the arts and sciences.

1757

Robert Clive of the British East
India Company won an important
battle. Many believe this was the
beginning of British control of India.

1947

India gained its independence from Great Britain.

2011

India won the Cricket World Cup.

2007

Pratibha Patil (*right*) became the first female president of India. In 1966, Indira Gandhi had become India's first female prime minister.

An Important Symbol

India's flag was adopted in 1947. It has three stripes. They are orange-yellow, white, and green. In the center of the white stripe is a **symbol**. It is called the Dharma Chakra, or wheel of the law.

India's government is a **federal republic**. The president is the head of state. The prime minister is the head of government. The country's laws are made by a parliament with two houses.

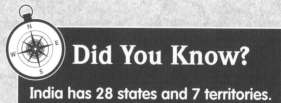

Did You Know?

India has 28 states and 7 territories.

The Dharma Chakra was used by Emperor Ashoka in the 200s BC. It is a very old symbol.

The two houses of India's parliament are the Lok Sabha and the Rajya Sabha. Both houses meet in the Parliament House (*left*).

ACROSS THE LAND

India has forests, beaches, mountains, and deserts. The snow-capped Himalayas are in the north. They are the highest mountains in the world! The Ganges and Brahmaputra Rivers flow through a large plain in the north.

It gets hot and cold in India. Most of India is hot and dry from March to June. A **monsoon** season brings rain and wind. It is from June to September. Most of India is cool and dry from October to February.

Did You Know?

Some parts of India are colder than other parts. In Darjeeling, the average yearly temperature is about 55°F (13°C). In Delhi, it is 79°F (26°C).

Cherrapunji is one of the wettest places on Earth. It is in northeastern India.

Many types of animals make their homes in India. These include Bengal tigers, monkeys, cobras, rhinoceroses, and elephants.

India has many kinds of plants. Lotuses, orchids, and marigolds grow there. India is also known for growing tea leaves and spice plants.

Did You Know?

Cattle are considered sacred by many of India's people.

The tiger is the country's national animal.

The lotus is India's national flower.

Earning a Living

India has many important businesses. The country's railway is run by the government. It is the largest **employer** in India. Many people also work in factories such as cotton, steel, and iron mills. Others work for electronics companies.

India also has natural **resources**. Coal and iron ore come from its mines. So do gold, silver, diamonds, and emeralds. Farmers produce rice, corn, and tea. Cattle and water buffalo are raised for their milk and hides.

India is a leading producer of bananas (*below*), mangoes, and a natural fiber called jute.

LIFE IN INDIA

India is known for its food, films, and music. Indian food uses spices such as cumin, mustard seeds, and red pepper. These can make food very spicy! India's film business is known around the world as Bollywood. Music from Indian films is very popular. People also listen to classical Indian songs.

There are different types of **transportation** in India. People get around in trains, buses, and cars. They also use motorcycles and bikes. Some ride in carts pulled by animals.

Did You Know?

In India, school is free for children ages 6 to 14.

India's food is often brightly colored! This is because of gold, orange, and red spices.

Music from Indian movies is known for being fun and upbeat.

Sports and games are popular in India. Favorites include cricket, field hockey, and football, or soccer. People also play chess and cards.

Most Indian people practice Hinduism. Hindus believe in many different gods and goddesses. They have **sacred** texts, objects, and animals. They may also visit temples and other special places to honor their religion.

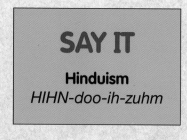

SAY IT

Hinduism
HIHN-doo-ih-zuhm

The Hindu temple in Tirupati is one of the most visited temples in India.

Flying kites is a favorite activity in India.

Famous Faces

Many famous people have lived in India. Mohandas Gandhi was born in Porbandar in 1869. Many people consider him the father of India. That's because he helped free India from British rule.

Gandhi was known for fighting for Indian rights. However, he did this without hurting anyone. Gandhi was killed in 1948. He is remembered for his peaceful work.

 **Did You Know?**

Gandhi also worked for Indian rights in South Africa.

Gandhi spent time in jail for sharing
his ideas. He believed this was okay in
order to teach people about his beliefs.

Blessed Mother Teresa was born in 1910 in Macedonia. Her given name was Agnes Gonxha Bojaxhiu. She became a nun around 1930. In 1948, she became an official citizen of India.

Mother Teresa spent much of her life teaching and working in what is now Kolkata. There, she found many hungry, sick, and poor people. She provided food and care for them. Mother Teresa was given many awards for her work. When she died in 1997, people around the world were saddened.

Mother Teresa was known as the "saint of the gutters." That's because she helped sick and poor people from the streets.

Tour Book

Have you ever been to India? If you visit the country, here are some places to go and things to do!

Discover

See the view from Tiger Hill near Ghoom. The Ghoom station is the highest railway station on the Darjeeling Himalayan Railway. It is near Kanchenjunga, which is the third-highest mountain in the world.

Explore

Watch fireworks during Diwali. This is also known as the Festival of Lights. It is a popular Hindu festival that lasts two to five days in October or November. People decorate their homes, exchange gifts, and light oil lamps.

🧭 Sip

Have a cup of tea in Darjeeling. This city is in the Himalayas. It is famous for growing tea leaves on large farms.

🧭 Play

Build a sand castle on one of the beaches in Goa! People go there to have fun and swim in the Arabian Sea.

🧭 See

Visit the city of Agra to see the Taj Mahal. Go up close to see the detailed decorations. People travel from all over the world to see this wonder. It took more than 20,000 workers to build it!

A GREAT COUNTRY

The story of India is important to our world. The people and places that make up this country offer something special. They help make the world a more beautiful, interesting place.

Gurudongmar Lake is one of the world's highest lakes! It is in the state of Sikkim near India's border with China.

37

India Up Close

Official Name: Bharat Ganarajya
(Republic of India)

Flag:

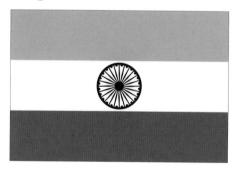

Population (rank): 1,205,073,612
(July 2012 est.)
(2nd most-populated country)

Total Area (rank): 1,269,219 square miles
(7th largest country)

Capital: New Delhi

Official Languages: Hindi, English

Currency: Indian rupee

Form of Government: Federal republic

National Anthem: "Jana-gana-mana"
(Thou Art the Ruler of the Minds of All People)

Important Words

capital a city where government leaders meet.
civilization a well-organized and advanced society.
dynasty (DEYE-nuh-stee) a powerful group or family that rules for a long time.
emperor the male ruler of an empire.
employer a person or company that pays people for their work.
federal republic a form of government in which the people choose the leader. The central
  government and the individual states share power.
monsoon a seasonal wind in southern Asia that sometimes brings heavy rain.
resource a supply of something useful or valued.
sacred (SAY-kruhd) connected with worship of a god.
symbol (SIHM-buhl) an object or mark that stands for an idea.
transportation the act of moving people or things from one place to another.

Web Sites

To learn more about India, visit ABDO Publishing Company online. Web sites about India are featured on our Book Links page. These links are routinely monitored and updated to provide the most current information available.

www.abdopublishing.com

Index